YOU HAVE

50 Myths About Islam

BY PROLIFIC AUTHOR:

Ismael Bilal Saleem I

Ismael Bilal Saleem II

ISBN-13:
978-1530397266

ISBN-10:
153039726X

Al-Qur'an 61:8 They want to extinguish the light of Allah with their mouths, but Allah will perfect His light, although the disbelievers dislike it.

CONTENTS

ACKNOWLEDGMENTS

First and foremost, Alhamdulillah. All praise is due to ALLAH. He is the source of all truth, therefore all that I convey of the truth in this book and in life are because of ALLAH, and only the mistakes are from me.

1. ALL MUSLIMS ARE ARABS:

Though Prophet Muhammad (pbuh) was an Arab and most of his first followers were Arab, not all Muslims are Arab and not all Arabs are Muslim. Islam is a way of life for all of mankind and it has been spread all over the world. In fact, there are 1.8 billion Muslims on earth and only 20% of them are Arabs. There are 7.27 million Muslims in North America, 600,000 Muslims in Oceania, 2.41 million Muslims in South America, 51.46 million Muslims in Europe, 1.215 billion Muslims in Asia and 509 million Muslims in Africa. Most Muslims are Asian. Islam is the largest religion in the continent of Africa with over 52% of the population. And Islam is the fastest growing religion in Europe and North America.

2. MUSLIMS DON'T BELIEVE IN JESUS (PBUH):

It is a central part of Islam for every Muslim to believe in the Prophets of God, including Abraham, Moses, David, Solomon and Jesus (pbut). As a Prophet of God, Jesus (pbuh) is considered to have a character that is exemplary and he is held in the ranks of the greatest men to have ever lived. He was chosen by God to deliver the message of Islam to the children of Israel. Muslims believe in the miraculous birth of Jesus (pbuh) and his many miracles. However Muslims do not believe Jesus (pbuh) to be God or the literal son of God (for more information see the book "There is no Trinity"). Muslims also reject the belief that Jesus' (pbuh) crucifixion and resurrection was a payment for the sins of mankind. It is the belief of Muslims that God saved His Prophet (pbuh) from the torturous and humiliating punishment on the cross (for more information see the book "Jesus was not Crucified"). Muslims love Jesus (pbuh), so much that many of them name themselves and their sons after him as he was a righteous man whose footsteps they would like to follow.

3. MUSLIMS WORSHIP MUHAMMAD (PBUH):

Islam is a strictly monotheistic religion. The belief in one God is essential to the religion and it is a tenet that cannot be compromised in any way. Muslims do not ascribe partners to God nor do they believe that God incarnates into human beings or animals. The holy book of Islam, the Qur'an, says that God is not begotten and He does not beget which means that He is not the son or the father of anyone. He has always existed and He will always exist and there is nothing comparable to God. There is no human being that could be or could have been God. There is no object that could be God. He is unimaginable. He is self-sustaining and He never sleeps nor does He feel weakness or fatigue. These things are explained to demonstrate that nothing and no one, including Muhammad (pbuh), can ever be God. Some have assumed that Christians worship Jesus (pbuh) and Buddhists worship Buddha (they do not), so Muslims must worship Muhammad (pbuh). However Muslims worship none but God. They only follow the example of Prophet Muhammad (pbuh).

4. ISLAM WAS SPREAD BY THE SWORD:

An often repeated but completely false charge is that Islam was spread by the sword. The Qur'an explicitly says that there is no compulsion in religion. Forcing someone to accept or to practice Islam is forbidden. Islam is to be spread through discussion, debate, reading (FROM MUSLIM SOURCES) and through the character and practices of Muslims. There have been many conquests by Muslims in history but none of these conquests were for the purpose of converting people to Islam. They were ignorable and abhorrent acts done by Muslims to gain power and wealth, but not to spread Islam. In fact, Muslims ruled Spain for 800 years. If Islam was spread by the sword, Spain would be a Muslim country, but the Muslims of that time were not interested in converts. They were interested in power. Arab Muslims were a part of the African slave trade. This was not to find new converts, but for wealth. Today more than half of Africa practices Islam, not because of the Muslim's sword, but they found Islam to be true despite the actions of some Muslims. In Saudi Arabia today, they are over 1 million people who are generational Christians since before the time of Prophet Muhammad (pbuh). If Islam was spread by the sword, they would not have been able to exist in a sea of Muslims. Indonesia, Africa, China, India, Britain and America have millions of Muslims living amongst them. Islam is the fastest growing religion in the world today. Which army persuaded these people to accept Islam? Islam is spread by the sword of truth.

WHAT NON-MUSLIMS HAVE TO SAY ABOUT THE ALLEGATION THAT ISLAM WAS SPREAD BY THE SWORD

1. M.K.GANDHI: "I became more than ever convinced that it was not the sword that won a place for Islam in those days in the scheme of life. It was the rigid simplicity, the utter self-effacement of the prophet, the scrupulous regard for his pledges, his intense devotion to his friends and followers, his intrepidity, his fearlessness, his absolute trust in God and in his own mission. These and not the sword carried everything before them and surmounted every trouble." YOUNG INDIA, 1924.

2. EDWARD GIBBON: "The greatest success of Mohammad's life was affected by sheer moral force without the stroke of a sword." HISTORY OF THE SARACEN EMPIRE, London, 1870.

3. A.S. TRITTON: "The picture of the Muslim soldier advancing with a sword in one hand and the Quran in

the other is quite false." ISLAM, London, 1951, page 21.

4. DE LACY O'LEARY: "History makes it clear however, that the legend of fanatical Muslims, sweeping through the world and forcing Islam at the point of sword upon conquered races is one of the most fantastically absurd myths that historians have ever repeated." ISLAM AT CROSSROADS, London, 1923, page 8.

5. K.S. RAMAKRISHNA RAO: "My problem to write this monograph is easier because we are not generally fed now on that (distorted) kind of history and much time need not be spent on pointing out our misrepresentations of Islam. The theory of Islam and sword, for instance, is not heard now in any quarter worth the name. The principle of Islam, there is no compulsion in religion, is well-known".
MOHAMMED THE PROPHET OF ISLAM, Riyadh 1989, page 4.

6. JAMES A. MICHENER. "No other religion in history spread so rapidly as Islam .... The West has widely believed that this surge of religion was made possible by the sword. But no modern scholar accepts that idea, and the Qur'an is explicit in support of the freedom of conscience." ISLAM THE MISUNDERSTOOD RELIGION, READERS DIGEST (American Edition) May 1955.

7. LAWRENCE E. BROWNE: "Incidentally these well-established facts dispose of the idea so widely fostered in Christian writings that the Muslims, wherever they went, forced people to accept Islam at the point of the sword." THE PROSPECTS OR ISLAM, London 1944.

5. MUSLIMS SEEK WORLD DOMINATION:

If you are on the internet for an extended period of time, you will come across a picture of a man with a sign reading "Islam Will Dominate the World." I don't claim to know this man's intentions, but I am sure that anti-Islam websites which plaster this image everywhere are doing so with the distinct aim at putting fear into the hearts and minds of non-Muslims. I have even heard popular televangelists use this same tactic. But they are mistaken or they are being dishonest with this depiction of Islam. As I have demonstrated, Islam was not spread by the sword, but very few non-Muslims know this fact. So when they are told about the idea that Muslims want to take over the world, it appears sinister. Many people fear that Islam's conversion rate will be a detriment to their ideology, so they play to the fears and prejudices of people. They consciously or unconsciously continue the lie told against Islam.

However, Islam has spread so vastly and so rapidly because it is the religion of truth. And truth should always dominate. When a Muslim wants the world to be Muslim, he is no different than a Christian who offers others Christianity, a Buddhist who offers others Buddhism, an Atheist offering others Atheism, or a Democratic country offering another country democracy. To each group, they have the truth and they feel that it should be shared with the world. And if they have the truth, of course most of the world is likely to accept it. May the best idea win.

6. MUSLIMS THINK THAT WHITE PEOPLE ARE THE DEVIL:

Due to the popularity of people like Malcolm X, Louis Farrakhan, Elijah Muhammad and the Nation of Islam (N.O.I.) in America, many people have become confused about the beliefs of orthodox Islam. The Nation of Islam is a sect of Islam that was formed in 1935 amongst the African American community during the time that they were experiencing extreme and overt forms of discrimination and racism. The Nation became a means to strengthen and empower the African American community in these times. However to achieve this goal, they altered the fundamental teachings of Islam and repackaged it as a religion for African Americans. They postulated that the Black man was god of the universe and that white people were evil people, i.e. devils. These ideas are far from the Islam taught 1400 years ago by Prophet Muhammad (pbuh). Islam is completely against racism. The Prophet Muhammad (pbuh) taught that all of mankind come from one soul, thus we are all brothers and sisters. It is God who made us different races, ethnicities, and tribes that we should get to know and understand one another.

7. ISLAM STARTED 1400 YEARS AGO:

It is a great misconception amongst non-Muslims and Muslims that Islam began around 610 A.D. with the revelations given to Prophet Muhammad (pbuh). Prophet Muhammad (pbuh) was the last of the prophets sent to mankind, which means that there were prophets that came before him. Islam maintains that Jesus, Ezekiel, Noah, Moses, Aaron, Joseph, Isaac, Abraham, Lot, Jonah, Job, Ishmael, Jacob, David, Solomon, Shua'ib, and many others were sent with the same message that Muhammad (pbut) conveyed. In fact, in Islam the first man, Adam (pbuh), was a prophet of Islam. The Qur'an says that prophets were sent to EVERY people with God's message and that message is SUBMISSION TO THE TRUE WILL OF GOD. In Arabic, the word *Islam* means submission to the will of God and one who submits to his will is a *Muslim*. When Moses (pbuh) told the Children of Israel to follow the laws of God, he was telling them to forsake their own will and submit to the will of God. When Noah (pbuh) told his people to get into the Ark, he was essentially saying, forsake your own will and submit to the will of God. Lot (pbuh) told the people of Sodom to resist their own desires and submit to the will of God. The men and women who took those prophets' advice were practicing Islam and they were

Muslims. When Adam (pbuh) submitted his will to God, he was a Muslim. When Jesus (pbuh) said "not as I will, but as you (God) will," this is an almost word for word definition of a Muslim. Therefore as long as there have been human beings, there has been Islam, but Islam goes even further than that. Not only do human beings follow Islam, but everything in existence submits to God. The grass grows as God has ordained it to. The sun shines as God ordains it to. The planets orbit the sun as God's law commands it to. Thus everything is in submission to the will of God. Everything is in a state of Islam. Everything, that is not God, is his creation and all of his creation submits to his will. Islam began as soon as God created the first thing. The universe is 13.8 billion years old. So Islam began AT LEAST 13.8 BILLION YEARS AGO.

8. THE NOBLE QUR'AN COPIED THE BIBLE:

One claim that is often alleged by non-Muslims is that the Qur'an, the Muslim Holy Book, is a copy or plagiarism of the Bible. The first point to be made is that the person making this claim has used the word *plagiarism* incorrectly. Plagiarism is

-the unauthorized use or close imitation of the language and thoughts of another author and the representation of them as one's own original work.

However the person making this accusation against the Qur'an wishes to say that Prophet Muhammad (pbuh) used the same CHARACTERS as the Bible and as you can see this is not in the definition of *plagiarism*. Also, Prophet Muhammad (pbuh) does not imitate the language or thoughts of the Bible, nor does he say that the Qur'an is his own work. The reason that the accuser uses words like *plagiarized, copied*, and *forged* is because they are more provocative, but these words are definitely inaccurate. The Qur'an says that it is a CORRECTION and COMPLETION from God (not Muhammad) of previous scriptures. Therefore when it used the same character as the Bible it is in order to correct, clarify or complete the story of this person. One cannot correct someone else without mentioning some of the same aspects of the story. For example, both the Quran and the Bible mention Jesus (pbuh) however the Qur'an explicitly says that Jesus (pbuh) is not the son of God and that he was not crucified, while the Bible maintains views which are the polar opposite. Is this copying? Not at all. It is the Qur'an correcting and clarifying people's ideas about Jesus (pbuh). The same is true for Moses, Abraham and all the prophets (pbut) mentioned in the Qur'an. The Bible says that Aaron (pbuh) made a golden calf for the Israelites to worship. The Qur'an says that this prophet of God did not violate God's most important law. The Qur'an, like the Bible, talks about the creation of the universe. However there are huge differences in their narrations. One difference is that the Bible says that God rested after creation, while the Qur'an says that no sleep or slumber can seize him. Is this plagiarism or correction? There are a multitude of examples to solidify this point. This topic is addressed in the book entitled "Islam is the Truth" and very specifically in the book entitled "The Jewish Torah is not the Word of God."

9. MUSLIMS ARE TERRORISTS:

It is a sad truth that many Muslims have used terrorism to gain attention for their cause, to scare their enemies or as a means of defense. Their practices have placed a stain upon Islam, but Islam is completely against the use of terrorism and suicide bombing. Suicide is a grave sin in Islam. It is one that cannot be repented for because the person committing suicide has died and one cannot repent and then commit the sin that they are repenting for. Also the Qur'an says that the murder of one person is as if you had murdered the whole of humanity. The Qur'an only allows for fighting in self-defense or in the defense of the weak and oppressed. There is no instance in which the Qur'an advocates or permits terrorism or aggression against non-Muslims despite the non-Muslims (and Muslims) claims to the contrary. EVERY SINGLE TIME the Qur'an speaks about fighting a specific group of people, it is speaking about that specific group at that time and it is in the realm of self-defense. For instance, the Qur'an says fight the disbelievers. Those who wish to slander Islam might quote this verse to suggest that Muslims must fight all disbelievers. However this is about a specific group who attacked Prophet Muhammad (pbuh) and his followers. Thus the Qur'an is encouraging Muslims to stand and fight and not to retreat in that instance. It would be like quoting a general from the American Revolution who said kill the British. Obviously, he meant kill the British that were fighting him in the American Revolution, not every British person who will ever live.

10. MUSLIMS HATE NON-MUSLIMS:

Muslims are told in the Qur'an to tell others about the religion of Islam, but what if the non-Muslim does not accept Islam? Are they forever enemies? Many people have the idea that Muslims have ill feelings towards non-Muslims for not accepting Islam. The first point to be made is that every non-Muslim is not a disbeliever. In the Qur'an, the Arabic word *kafir* is usually translated as disbeliever. *Kafir* carries the meaning of one who hides and rejects the truth of Islam. They are those who have had Islam clearly presented to them, they understand its validity and they continue to reject it. They are like a criminal who knows that it is wrong and against the law to steal, but they do it anyway for they own reasons. So when one reads about a disbeliever in the Qur'an, this is the person that it is speaking of, not simply anyone who does not believe in Islam. But if the Muslim propagates his faith to someone and they do not believe, he is to tell the non-Muslim, "you keep your way of life and I will keep mine." The Muslim and the non-Muslim can be friends, partners and patrons of one another. Muslims are taught to respect other people's beliefs. But Muslims are told not to befriend non-Muslims who make a mockery of Islam and those who try to force Muslims to change their religion.

Also Muslims are not to get their religious and spiritual guidance from none other than his fellow Muslims. Only God knows what is in the hearts of man, so it should not be a Muslim's prerogative to treat non-Muslims unfairly because they will not accept Islam.

11. ISLAM OPPRESSES WOMEN:

Perhaps the most controversial and divisive topic of discussion in Islam is the role and treatment of women. It must first be stated that women have all the religious obligations that a man has, which means she also has the same reward and punishment for her good and bad deeds. In anticipation for the question of equality between men and women, God makes it abundantly clear that the pillars and moral conduct of Islam is for every adult, male and female.

Al-Qur'an 33:35 For Muslim men and women,- for believing men and women, for devout men and women, for true men and women, for men and women who are patient and constant, for men and women who humble themselves, for men and women who give in Charity, for men and women who fast (and deny themselves), for men and women who guard their chastity, and for men and women who engage much in Allah's praise,- for them has Allah prepared forgiveness and great reward.

And believing men and women are protecting friends of one another. They aid and guide each other into righteousness (9:71). So, women's religious duties are the same as men's duties, but what about their social life? When pondering this topic, it is best to strip away all preconceived ideas and get our guidance from the Qur'an. Taking this approach, it becomes impossible to justify the treatment of women in much of the Muslim world. However there is a sharp contract between culture and religion. Yet these lines are blurred so often when discussing Islam that the distinction is rarely made between the two. Female circumcision/mutilation, women walking behind men, and women prevented from driving cars are all examples of culture being mistaken for Islam. None of these things are to be found in the pages of the Qur'an. So before an allegation is made, it must be shown to be a part of Islam and not simply a practice performed by Muslims.

In the times of Prophet Muhammad (pbuh), it was more preferable to have a son than a daughter. Many parents were upset when the new addition to the family was female. Yet Prophet Muhammad (pbuh) denounced such behavior. He maintained that a female's birth is as equal a blessing as a male's birth. But this was not simply a problem of preference. The practice of female infanticide was implemented for those unsatisfied with their newborn baby girl. The Arabs used to bury their daughters alive. To extinguish this grave sin, Prophet Muhammad (pbuh) outlawed infanticide (16:58-59). The Qur'an also makes mention that those who practiced such brutality will have to face the consequences of their deeds in the hereafter (81:8-9). This is to show that Islam directly impacted the life of women in a dramatically positive way. Before women could fight for their civil rights, Muhammad (pbuh) fought for their right to live. He fought for their right to be treated with fairness and with the love that a parent would have bestowed upon a male child. Not only did he fight for their rights, but when Islam became the religion of Arabia, he won them their rights and their right to live. He saved thousands, if not millions of women's lives. But instead of Muhammad (pbuh) being respected and praised for his efforts to emancipate women from this barbarism, he is most often vilified for propagating sexism.

In Islam, men and women are to dress modestly to avoid attention from the opposite sex unless it is their spouse. The Qur'an says that Muslim women "should cast their outer garments over their persons" so to avoid accentuating their body parts (33:59). This is to distinguish chaste Muslim women from any other women on the street and to avoid harassment from other men. The veil or modest dress is not oppression of women. It is incorporated for the exact same reason that nuns are dressed the way that they are. It is a testament to their belief and devotion to GOD. And in the case of the Muslim woman, it is also a testament of devotion to her husband. It is a sign of dignity and respect for themselves, that they do not wish for or need the adulation of anyone other than their husbands. All the great women of faith dressed in this manner, yet it is eschewed in today's society as oppressive while skimpy dress is encouraged.

Women today go to work or the marketplace, with a bit of cleavage showing and tight fitting jeans to display their figure. Then they come home to their husband and get comfortable. They take off all the clothing that restricts their blood circulation and put on a huge t-shirt and jogging pants. They are doing the exact opposite of what the GOD says and what the sensible thing to do is. They are showing the world their goods and covering up for their husband. These are the same women who are offended when random men are disrespectful to them on the street and whose husband pay them little attention. You can take the advice of society at large or you can take the advice of Him who created the society at large. It is your choice. Fortunately in recent years there have been a large number of converts to Al-Islam in America and the majority of these converts are women. They are beginning to understand that modest dress is not oppressive. It is in fact the skimpy dressing that is the means by which women are objectified and oppressed.

12. MUSLIMS BELIEVE IN THE BIBLE:

Unfortunately many Muslims and non-Muslims believe that the Bible is a book of authority in Islam. The Bible is a book which Muslims should read and study, but it cannot and should not be adhered to in the same manner as Muslims adhere to the Qur'an. This myth finds its root in some people's misunderstanding of the Qur'an. The Qur'an speaks very highly of the Taurat, the Injil, and the Zabur. These revelations are translated into English as the Torah, the Gospel and the Psalms. The Qur'an says that the Prophet Moses (pbuh) received the Torah from God, the Prophet Jesus (pbuh) received the Gospel from God and the Prophet David (pbuh) received the Psalms from God. But the Qur'an also warns us that there are people who write books and falsely attribute them to God. What we must understand is that these revelations were given to these Prophets of God (pbut); however they are not what exist in the Bible today. And one does not have to take a Muslim's word for it. Pick up any Bible and check for the author of the Torah, the Psalms and the Gospels and you will find that Moses, David and Jesus (pbut) did not author these books attributed to them.

Of course, no one attributes the Gospels of the New Testament to Jesus (pbuh), yet these gospels mention that Jesus (pbuh) went from place to place preaching the GOSPEL. Muslims do not believe in the gospel according to Matthew, Mark, Luke or John, which are his biographies. We believe in the Gospel according to Jesus (pbuh), i.e. whatever he went from place to place preaching. Likewise, we believe in the actual preaching and teachings of Moses and David (pbut) which are called the Torah and the Psalms. Yet you will be hard-pressed to find any Biblical scholar, whether Jewish or Christian, that accepts the claim that these Bible books are authored by Moses and David (pbut). The real Torah and Psalms have yet to be found, if ever. They were most likely oral traditions.

13. THE QUR'AN HAS MANY DIFFERENT VERSIONS:

It has been the proclivity of some Christian apologists to assert that Muslims have many different versions of the Qur'an, just as Christians have many versions of the Bible. This is a huge myth. The Bible has the King James VERSION, the American Standard VERSION, the New International VERSION, the Douay-Rheims VERSION,etc. A version is

-a description or account from one point of view, especially as opposed to another

They are called versions because they say different things on the same issue. Some of these versions of the Bible have a word or two that another version doesn't have. Some have a phrase or two that another version doesn't have. Some have a sentence or two. Some have a verse or two. Some have a chapter or two that another version does not have. Some of these versions of the Bible have 73 books in them, while others have 66 books. You see this is not merely a matter of translation. To translate is

-to render in another language

Some of the versions of the Bible are so different that it changes the tenets of one's belief in Christianity, even in terms of God and Jesus (pbuh). At any rate, the Qur'an has many different translations, not

33

different versions. Different translators use different English words to convey the Arabic of the Qur'an, but all the Arabic in the Qur'ans are the same. The reason the Bible has so many versions is because they have literally thousands of manuscripts that they form their Bibles from, but none of these Hebrew, Greek and Aramaic manuscripts are identical. They all have varying details, thus making the existence of differing versions of the Bible inevitable. Fortunately, the Qur'an has been well preserved.

"It is as it was 1400 years ago, which a Muslim can verify by comparing his Qur'an with that of the two existing Qur'ans in the city of Tashkent of Uzbekistan and Istanbul of Turkey. This preservation is also a fulfilled prophecy in the Qur'an."

Al-Qur'an 15:9 We have, without doubt, sent down the Message; and We will assuredly guard it (from corruption). {In Arabic, there is a plural for numbers and a plural used to demonstrate sovereignty and majesty. The Qur'an uses this plural of majesty for God in this verse.}
-*Islam is the Truth*, I.D. Campbell

14. DEATH FOR LEAVING ISLAM:

The penalty of death for apostasy is false and contrary to the teachings of the Qur'an. Belief is something inside of you. It is how you are convinced of a certain thing. It is different for everyone. Your *iman* or confirmation grows as you live and study Islam. This cannot be measured by man, which is why the Qur'an leaves it to God to regulate apostasy, unless your disbelief causes you to harm others. All the verses of the Qur'an dealing with someone who changes his mind about his faith in Islam speak of ALLAH punishing him, not man because only ALLAH knows a man's heart and intentions. These verses speak of people who believe, then disbelieve over and over again, but every time, they can be forgiven if they sincerely repent before they die. ALLAH is not harmed in the least bit. He will simply substitute them for those who are firm in their belief. So it is not necessary to kill someone for changing their mind.

The Qur'an also speaks of Muslims who, under compulsion, denounce Islam. It stipulates that a Muslim, if threaten, has an option to proclaim his belief or claim unbelief (16:106). Of course, this is an example of why man must not persecute others for their decision to accept or reject Islam, because they have no idea what is in the heart of another man.

15. ALLAH IS A MOON GOD:

If a person has the same name as someone else or if a person mistakenly gave someone the name that is rightfully due to someone else, this in no way, shape or form affects the actual person or being who the name describes. Any rational person will acknowledge this fact, but there are those who go out of their way to discredit Islam with pitiful arguments like Arabs use to call the moon-god ALLAH, thus Muslims today are worshipping the moon-god.

The Arabs despite their worship of a multitude of gods, even before the birth of Prophet Muhammad (pbuh), held ALLAH as the supreme deity. ALLAH was viewed as the Hindus view the Brahman, above description. And like the Hindus, they allocated inferior deities to bridge the gap between them and the supreme God. But there have been some Christian opponents of Islam, who suggest that the Arabs called one of these lesser gods, ALLAH. Of course, this is unsubstantiated and refuted by Muslim scholars who prove the moon god which they are referring to was actually called Sin, not ALLAH.
-
(http://www.islamicawareness.org/Quran/Sources/Alla h/moongod.html)

But even if their claim is true, they shoot themselves in the foot, when they say that ALLAH is but a contraction of AL-ILAH which is "the God" in Arabic. They have to dissect the word "ALLAH" to have any point to make, because as I have said Arabs have been calling the supreme God, ALLAH forever. Even Arab Christians called God ALLAH before Muhammad (pbuh) brought Islam. It becomes obvious that the generic word for god, "*ilah*," could have been used for every single god that they had. So they play a sad game of associating the word "*ilah*" with the Canaanite god "Baal." The first problem that they have is Baal was the sun-god, when they said ALLAH is the moon god. The second problem that they have is that "*ilah*" is related to the Hebrew word "*el*," which is used in the Bible for the Hebrew God. This means that the word used for God in the Bible is subject to the same criticism as the word for God in Arabic, i.e. they too worship the moon-god (or sun god). And a third problem is that in the mythology of Baal the sun-god, his father was named "EL." In fact, the words "Baal" and "el" were interchangeable until a rift came between the Jews and the Canaanites.

Also, the polytheistic Moabites used Yahweh or Jehovah as the name of God, and even early Jews gave Yahweh, a wife name Asherah. If the discrepancies of people of the past, including Israelites, do not discredit the validity of the God of the Jews and Christians, then the discrepancy of the past Arabs have no bearing on the God of Islam. Furthermore, no Muslim worships any earthly or heavenly body. This point is brought home by the Quran itself.

Al-Qur'an 41:37 Among His Signs are the Night and the Day, and the Sun and the Moon. Do not prostrate to the sun and the moon, but prostrate to Allah, Who created them, if it is Him ye wish to serve.

16. MUSLIMS HATE JEWS:

One myth which frequently repeats itself is that Islam is an anti-Semitic religion. The first point to be made is that Arabs are a Semitic people; as such Prophet Muhammad (pbuh) was a Semite. And the majority of the prophets mentioned in the Qur'an are from the house of Israel, i.e. Semites. Therefore it is rather ridiculous to call a religion which has an abundance of Semitic prophets anti-Semitic.

The second point is that Muslims and Jews have a conflict with each other over the land called Israel. This rift is a rather recent development. Muslims and Jews have lived in relative peace for centuries until this current dilemma. In fact, Jews often escaped to Muslim lands to seek refuge from their enemies seeking to kill them.

The final point is the Qur'an recounts the abundance of blessings the Children of Israel were granted from God and their multiple transgressions against God. If this qualifies as anti-Jewish, then it is quite mild in comparison to the Jewish Torah's account on the same issue. The Jewish Torah on numerous occasions cited God's anger with the Children of Israel, to such an extent that he regretted making man and he sought to wipe out the whole of humanity. Yet the Qur'an calls for Muslims to give the greatest gift that they have to the Jews, his religion of truth, Islam. The fact that all Muslims want all Jews to be one with them as Muslims, not for political gain or material gain, but solely for the benefit of his Jewish brother, is the ultimate proof that the Muslim is not anti-Semitic, in any sense of the word.

17. THE IMPORTANCE OF PORK:

One of the best known principles of Islam is that it prohibits the consumption of pork. Ask a person on the street what does he know about Islam, he may have all kinds of crazy ideas about Islam, but he knows for certain that Muslims can't eat pork. Of course, he is correct in this matter. The Qur'an forbids Muslims from eating pork, unless there are circumstances which necessitates that you eat it. For those who have eaten pork all of their lives, it seems like a hard task, but it really isn't. There are plenty of foods that one can eat besides pork, that taste great and are healthier for you. But the issue is the importance that non-Muslims place on pork.

Because they place so much stock in pork consumption, they mislead themselves into thinking that abstaining from pork is a pillar of Islam. It is a tenet of Islam, but not the root for which Islam is built upon. Of greater importance is the belief in One God and His prophet Muhammad (pbuh). Some dismiss Islam because they "can't stop eating pork," as if this precedes belief in One God, in Muhammad (pbuh) and the Qur'an. No, first you understand Islam and you believe in God, in Muhammad (pbuh) and in the Qur'an and then you will follow the tenets of Islam. This is how all of your actions are performed. First is belief and then there is action. You believe if you place one foot in front of the other, you will start walking, so you do it. You believe that when you place your key into the ignition of your car that the car will start, so you do it. First you believe that pork is not good for you and God has ordained that you abstain from it and then you eliminate it from your diet.

18. ISLAM PROMOTES POLYGAMY:

The Qur'an adamantly promotes marriage and monogamy between a man and a woman. However, the Qur'an does allow for polygamy in special circumstances. Though it is presented by Muslims and non-Muslims oftentimes as a very important part of Islam, polygamy is not a widely practiced part of the religion. In fact, it is not prescribed but permitted in circumstances like the aftermath of a war where men are scarce. Today a very small percentage of Muslims practice polygamy, between 2 and 5%. This is a testament to how prevalent the circumstances arise which allow for polygamy. Of course, the women involved decide whether this is suitable for them and some women have as a stipulation in their marriage dower that they will not be a part of any polygamous relationship. As an extremely practical religion, Islam has the solution for all the problems of mankind, including a means by which a woman can remain chaste in times of a scarcity of men. This solution is in sharp contrast to a woman having to lead a life of celibacy, having to be a mistress or being one amongst many other women who can LAWFULLY be with one man as long as he does NOT make a commitment and oath to be with them forever in marriage in Western society.

19. ISLAM WAS CREATED BY THE VATICAN:

One myth that has been gaining momentum on the internet is that Islam was created by the Vatican. This conspiracy theory is completely unfounded and completely fabricated. Its conception began in the mind of Christian Fundamentalist author Jack Chick and it was promoted by Alberto Rivera. Rivera was known for his dishonesty through his legal troubles which included theft and fraud, as well as writing bad checks. Rivera wrote a bad check on Islam and many people eager to discredit Islam have tried to cash it.

Both Chick and Rivera were noted anti-Catholic activists. They attributed Catholicism with everything from the Holocaust to the rise of Communism. Not only did Chick allege that the Catholic Church created Islam, but he also asserts that they started the Mormon Church and the Jehovah's Witness movement.

As it pertains to Islam, it has been previously noted that Islam began before the start of humanity, thus Mr. Chick and Mr. Rivera are in need of a Catholic Church which was present before humanity began. Furthermore, Islam has specific tenets which not only contradict Catholicism but corrects it. Islam maintains that all prophets were Muslims, that God does not beget a son, that he is not begotten, that Jesus (pbuh) was only a prophet and that he was not crucified. Why would the Vatican create a religion which calls the cornerstone of their beliefs into question? Just recently, it was declared that Islam has overtaken Catholicism in terms of its following. Why would Catholics create a system which would overtake Catholicism? In short, this accusation is a concoction of Mr. Chick and Mr. Rivera's imagination.

A former follower and admirer of Jack Chick by the name of Gary Dale Cearley has written a book entitled "Thou Shall Not Bear False Witness: The Truth about the Vatican and the Birth of Islam" which debunks the claim that the Vatican created Islam entirely. Here are a few quotes from Mr. Cearley:

"These vicious lies by Jack Chick and his cohorts have gone on far, far too long."

"They claim to be lovers of God but it is impossible to love God and not respect the truth."

"Jack Chick was a real Christian in my mind when I was young but my whole opinion of him changed when I started receiving e-mails containing the story line 'How the Vatican Created Islam'. I saw immediately that Chick, through the testimony of this fraud Alberto Rivera, was intent (on) defaming two faiths at the expense of historical truths. So I became impassioned. I had to publicly refute the whole bogus story."

http://www.prleap.com/pr/41942/

20. "ALLAHU AKBAR" IS A WAR CRY:

Time and time again, the news and movies depict an Arab man performing or speaking of a terrorist act and the man begins chanting "ALLAHU AKBAR." This image has left some with the impression that "ALLAHU AKBAR" is sort of a war chant which is screamed in acts of violence or even when contemplating such acts. This scene has been repeated so often that it can no longer be considered a coincidence.

The Arabic words "ALLAHU AKBAR" are translated as "GOD IS THE GREATEST" but it literally means "ALLAH or God is greater." It is an incomplete phrase, because it is left up to anyone to complete it. The idea is that you can use anything to finish the phrase and it will ultimately mean "God is greater *than whatever you can imagine,*" thus he is the greatest. As you can see, this phrase has absolutely nothing to do with terror or violence in any way. It is similar to a Christian saying "HALLELUJAH" to express their feelings of joy. Simply because some Muslims use it in error does not discount almost 2 billion Muslims using ALLAHU AKBAR a multitude of times during their 5 daily prayers. Even the Muslims' call to prayer has ALLAHU AKBAR in it six times, but of course prayer does not make the news.

21. JIHAD IS A HOLY WAR:

The Arabic word *jihad* means struggle. This struggle can be an inner struggle or an external struggle. The external struggle can be fighting in the cause of ALLAH or simply the struggle to propagate Islam to others.

Al-Quran 2:207 And there is the type of man who gives his life to earn the pleasure of Allah: And Allah is full of kindness to (His) devotees.

Malcolm X was a Muslim man who gave his life for the spread of the truth of Islam and though he never fought in war, he is a Muslim martyr. Ahmed Deedat, though he was not killed, he gave his life in another way to the spread of Islam. Both these men's lives were in a state of *jihad*. They were *mujahideen* or those who practice *jihad*. *Jihad* can be implored by force in terms of self-defense, or by your words and deeds to spread Islam. If a Muslim is incapable of speaking out or defending himself against injustice, the lowest form of *jihad* is to hate sin in your heart.

But the most important *jihad* is the one which the Muslim has with himself. In fact, he cannot struggle with the world, until he has first grappled with the instinct and urges inside of himself. Though the internal struggle is ever-present, it is controllable by man. He struggles daily to be righteous and to do what is best and resist what it wrong. In all, *jihad* is not a holy war, but an internal and external struggle to do what is right. In this sense, everyone is a *mujahid* or one who struggles.

22. ALLAH IS NOT A LOVING GOD:

Al-Quran 85:14 And He (Allah) is the Oft-Forgiving, Full of Loving-Kindness

I want this verse to be set into people's minds because it is something that should be on the lips of every Muslim today. Almost every non-Muslim in the world today thinks of ALLAH as some tyrannical, blood craving vengeful God, when this is the furthest from the truth. Because their knowledge of Islam is from those who are already prejudice against Islam, they have a poor understand of the God of Islam. God's love is spoken of in the Qur'an as being expressed through action.

Love is demonstrated through ALLAH'S provision, forgiveness, mercy and blessing that he bestows on ALL OF MANKIND, good or bad. The term "oft-forgiving" means that GOD repeatedly forgives man and that his love and kindness are in great abundance. 114 times the phrase *"BISMILLAHI RAHMANI RAHEEM"* is repeated in the Qur'an. It means "In the name of ALLAH, MOST GRACIOUS, MOST MERCIFUL." In Arabic, the words *"Rahman"* and *"Raheem"* have the same root *RHM* which means love or compassion. *Rahman* means that ALLAH'S love is so abundant that it is given to all his creation, whether they are deserving or not.

23. THE QUR'AN AND THE HADITHS HAVE THE SAME VALUE:

I visit different anti-Islamic websites and a common misconception is that the Qur'an and the traditions of the Prophet Muhammad (pbuh) known as the Hadiths are equivalent in nature, in status, and in importance. This is completely untrue, though many Muslims have similar views. The Qur'an is the actual revelation and words God put into the mouth of the Prophet Muhammad (pbuh). The Hadiths are the recorded actions and deeds of Prophet Muhammad and his close followers. Prophet Muhammad (pbuh) was the Qur'an in action. The Hadiths are very important to Islam. In them are the verbatim details of prayer, fasting, charity, the pilgrimage and many other important tenants of Islam. However all Hadiths are not authentic. Being transmitted from person to person and recorded long after the Prophets death, there are many discrepancies in the narrated stories of the Prophet Muhammad (pbuh). However there are absolutely no discrepancies in the Qur'an. The Qur'an is the criteria by which we measure the truth in all books, including the Hadiths. As a matter of fact, the Hadiths record Prophet Muhammad (pbuh) as saying that there will be fabricated stories about him, so make sure to measure these stories using the Qur'an.

In the Bible, we find that Jesus (pbuh) went to one city preaching the Gospel. Then he went to another city preaching the Gospel. But the Gospel he was preaching was not The Gospel of Matthew, Mark, Luke or John. All the words Jesus (pbuh) spoke were revelation directly from God, but the Gospels of Matthew, Mark, Luke and John are the recorded actions and deeds of the Prophet Jesus (pbuh). They are his Hadiths. In fact, the entire Bible is Hadiths or traditions of the different Prophets. They contain mistakes and contradictions because they are the words of men verbally transmitted numerous years after the events took place. These men wrote with their own bias, their own judgment, their own opinion and their own prejudice. Prophets of God (pbut) are oftentimes depicted in the most despicable light. The most heinous crimes are attributed to Prophets of God in their Hadiths (the Bible). Muslims believe these tales about the Prophets of God (pbut) to be untrue. And there were many things attributed to the Prophet Muhammad (pbuh) which are untrue. Fortunately, Muslims have the advantage of having the literal words of God which affirms that God chose these great men of exemplary character, because of their exemplary character. All the prophets were models for mankind to follow. Their character was far from the image that they are attributed in some of the stories about them.

There are thousands of traditions for the Prophet Muhammad (pbuh). In some of them, you may find errors in logic and reasoning, you may find mistakes, you may find scientific errors, you will find 72 virgins in Paradise, and death for apostasy and adultery. But you will find none of these things in the Qur'an. So the Hadiths which agree with the Qur'an are authentic. When you see someone talking disparagingly about The Prophet of Islam, ask him, "Where does it say that in the Qur'an?"

24. ISLAM IS LIKE OTHER RELIGIONS, IT DEMANDS BLIND FAITH:

Iman is often translated as faith in the Qur'an. Faith insinuates a belief in something without proof. This is not the definition of "*iman*." *Iman* means confirmation and acceptance of the truth. It is belief in something because you have proof. This is why the *mu'min*, translated as "believer," does not doubt anymore (49:15). So a believer is not the best translation for *mu'min*, but "someone with confirmation of the truth" may be more accurate. Repeatedly the Qur'an asks its reader to reflect, research, and investigate its content. It often speaks of "*iman* with certainty" (44:7, 45:4, 45:20), to illustrate that this is not faith but confirmation and understanding of the truth. All these verses cited speak of the Qur'an and its content as giving evidence and proof for your belief in God, in the Qur'an and in Islam. There is no such thing as certain faith. Certainty implies knowledge. In short, one should not be a Muslim because he was raised that way, or because it sounds good, but because he has come to the conclusion of his investigation to find that Islam is the religion of truth.

25. ISLAM SANCTIONS CHILD MARRIAGE:

One of Prophet Muhammad's (pbuh) wives which raise eyebrows was said to be a child by the name of Aisha. Wherever you find an avid anti-Islamist, you will find this issue rose. I do not fault them for bringing up this issue, because upon hearing this claim, I was in awe that anyone would believe it. I did not recall this being in the Qur'an, but I told myself that if it is in there then I do not believe or accept it. Fortunately, I found that it was, like all the other accusations, nowhere to be found in the Qur'an, but in the Hadiths. In the Hadiths, it says that Prophet Muhammad (pbuh) married Aisha when she was six years old and he consummated the marriage when she was nine years old. I have heard and read every kind of explanation for this marriage, but there is absolutely no explanation that will suit me.

The Hadiths are supposed to be the explanation of the Qur'an, but there is no mention of marriage and sex with children in it. One problem is that there are different accounts of how old Aisha was in the Hadiths, so it is inaccurate or deceitful to assert definitively that she was six years old. There are Hadiths presenting Aisha's age at the time of marriage to be from 6 to 21 years old. To say definitive that she was 6 years old is a deception, when she was 6, 7, 8, 9, 10, 11, 12, 13, 14, 15, 16, 17, 18, 19, 20 or 21. And I would like to know how non-Muslims discern which Hadiths to believe in. Do they accept the remaining Hadiths as truthful as well which say that Muhammad (pbuh) was a prophet of God and the Qur'an is the words of God?

The honest answer about her age is that a reliable source for her age does not exist. And the Qur'an makes no mention of it. Prophet Muhammad (pbuh) didn't marry a child because the Qur'an says a man can't marry a woman against her will (4:19), and a child has no will worth mentioning in this matter. The Qur'an also says that Prophet Muhammad (pbuh) had to choose between certain "women" (33:50, 33:52) as to who he would marry. And the Qur'an says that his wives were not like any other "women" (33:32). They were to be like Prophet Muhammad (pbuh), exemplary figures for the Muslim women. Prophet Muhammad (pbuh), as the ruler of Arabia at this time, offered them the option of living a lavish life of wealth, possessions and independence or the duty of following the path of Al-Islam. He informed them that their every action would be, as his was, a personification of Al-Islam. They were to be role models. And with this responsibility came an abundance of reward or an abundance of punishment from God (33:27-3). His wives accepted the hard road of Al-Islam over the easy path of riches. I ask, would this decision be given to a six or nine year old girl? And would a child not take money over prayer and fasting?

This allegation against Prophet Muhammad (pbuh), just simply makes no sense. The Qur'an says that in Paradise, the believers will be given companions of equal age to them (78:33). Thus the ideal marriage in Al-Islam is couples whose ages are in close proximity to each other. Again the marriage between Prophet Muhammad (pbuh) and a child is not exemplary to God's message. And the nail in the coffin is that Muhammad's (pbuh) wives were the "MOTHERS OF THE MUSLIMS" (33:6). How exactly does a grown man seek any kind of advice and comfort from his 9 year old mother?

With this, I conclude that the Qur'an is declaring that all of Prophet Muhammad's (pbuh) wives were adults capable of making sound decisions and giving sound advice. Thus Prophet Muhammad's (pbuh) marriage to a child would be against the teaching of the Qur'an.

26. MUSLIM MEN CAN BEAT THEIR WIVES:

When discussing the steps that a husband should take when he finds that his wife is guilty of ill-conduct or disloyalty most translations of the Quran say that he can "beat her (lightly)" or something to that effect (4:34). The Arabic word used here is "*adribu*" (root: *daraba*) and it means to beat, to strike, to hit, to separate, to part. The word is used in all these different forms in the Quran. The translators of the Quran have deemed "to beat" to be the best fit for the verse in question. But since the Quran is fully detailed, it explains itself (6:114). In another chapter, the Quran again speaks about this troubled marriage and it says that the couple is to separate for four months and after this separation, they can decide to return or to divorce.

Al-Qur'an 2:226 For those who take an oath for abstention from their wives, a waiting for four months is ordained; if then they return, Allah is Oft-forgiving, Most Merciful.

Al-Qur'an 2:227 But if their intention is firm for divorce, Allah heareth and knoweth all things.

Notice here that no beating is involved in this process. One does not abstain from being with his wife then come back to beat her, and then decide if he wants to reconcile or divorce. The four months is clearly a time to reflect on the marriage and to come to a rational decision. And if we look at the steps logically, it is clear that the word "*adribu*" should be translated as "separate from her" and not as "beat her."

Step 1. Admonish them (the couple is still together)

Step 2. Refuse to sleep in the same bed (the couple is still together)

Step 3. Beat your wife??? (the couple is still together)

The problem with this translation is the verse that succeeds this one.

Al-Qur'an 4:35 If ye fear a breach between them twain, appoint (two) arbiters, one from his family, and the other from hers; if they wish for peace, Allah will cause their reconciliation: For Allah hath full knowledge, and is acquainted with all things.

This verse is directed towards a concerned person on the outside of the relationship. It is apparent that this person fears that the couple will divorce, so this third party is to try to reconcile the couple. This would only make sense if the third step was that the couple separated (for four months) and the third party felt that divorce was the inevitable result of this separation. If the man beats his wife, then there is no mention of separation. So how can they get BACK TOGETHER?

The Qur'an says that husband and wife are to live on equitable terms (4:19). This means if the translator was to assume that a husband can beat his wife, then a wife can beat her husband, which I am sure he will not agree with because later on in this chapter, the wife of a husband who commits disloyalty and ill-conduct, has the permission that a husband has in the same situation (4:128). Also the Qur'an says that a man is to treat his wife with kindness and not to treat her harshly or keep her against her will (4:19). Beating your wife to get her to do as you wish is contrary to all these principles of the Qur'an. Hopefully, Muslims will unite and change this translation and put an end to the idea that wife-beating is acceptable in Al-Islam.

Note: An author by the name of Yahiya Emerick has printed three English Qur'ans, "The Holy Qur'an: Guidance for Life," "The Holy Qur'an in Today's English," and "A Journey through the Holy Qur'an," with the translation as "separate from your wife" instead of "beat your wife."

27. "WE" MEANS TRINITY:

Many Christians have been under the impression that the usage of "We" and "Us" in the Qur'an is indicative of the Trinity. First, "WE" doesn't necessarily imply Trinity. It could mean two or four or one thousand, so the argument is already invalid. Second, the people who make this argument seem to forget that the Qur'an was revealed in Arabic, which is a Semitic language, not English. In the Semitic languages there is a plural of numbers and a plural of respect used for high authorities such as kings. The Qur'an uses this plural of respect when mentioning God. This is why none of Prophet Muhammad's (pbuh) detractors ever accused him of polytheism.

28. MUSIC IS FORBIDDEN IN ISLAM:

A growing idea that many Muslims seem to adopt is that music is strictly forbidden. They get this from both the Hadith and a certain verse of the Qur'an which they have misinterpreted. I will focus only on the Qur'an because authentic Hadiths should agree with the Qur'an.

Al-Qur'an 31.6 But there are, among men, those who purchase idle tales, without knowledge (or meaning), to mislead (men) from the path of Allah...

Some scholars have interpreted "Idle tales/Idle talks" to mean music, but that clearly isn't the case. The word used for idle is "lahwa" which means pointless or for amusement, the word for talks is oddly enough "hadithi" as in "hadith" which means tales or speeches. Notice that neither of these words means music, and even if they did, notice that it says "among men" meaning there are only some people who do this so it's only potentially evil. For example, people use weapons to murder other people unjustifiably. Does that then mean you can't have a weapon? Of course not. The verse is saying, do not use idle talk to mislead people, which is clearly a sin. This does not pertain to music. How can a sound from drums or a flute or a piano be idle tales? The Arabic word for "music" is "musiqaa" and it is not mentioned in this verse at all. The lyrics of a song could be seen as idle tales used to mislead people, but that does not suggest that all lyrics are used in this way. Surely they are not. So the lyrics of a song which are used to mislead people are those which are forbidden.

29. ALLAH MISGUIDES PEOPLE INTO HELL:

What the people who make this argument tend to do is ignore the context of the verse that they are quoting. If you read the Qur'an carefully, you'll see who ALLAH is referring to when it says that He misguides.

Al-Qur'an 2:26 By it He causes many to stray, and many He leads into the right path; but He causes not to stray, except those who forsake (the path)

In other words, Allah misguides people who are already astray not just random people for any reason. So technically, ALLAH is leaving them astray, since they are already rebellious. Remember that a disbeliever is one who knows the truth and continues to reject it. Thus leaving them astray is a punishment for their sin and disbelief. Yet there is still hope for them.

Al-Qur'an 5:16 Wherewith Allah guideth all who seek His good pleasure to ways of peace and safety, and leadeth them out of darkness, by His will, unto the light,- guideth them to a path that is straight.

30. ALLAH IS AN EGOTISTICAL GOD WHO DEMANDS WORSHIP AND PRAISE:

I find it quite ironic how people say ALLAH should be independent when ALLAH himself says that he is free from wants in NUMEROUS PLACE IN THE QURAN (Surah 2:263, Surah 14:8, Surah 35:15, Surah27:40, etc.). The word ALLAH uses to describe himself in these verses is "Ghaniyyun" which means Rich, self-sufficient, and independent. Of course, this raises the question "what's the point of worshiping ALLAH?" The answer is that life is a test (Surah 18:7, Surah 21:35, Surah 27:47, Surah 3:185) to see which of us are best in conduct (Surah 67:2). And to do good deeds entails worshipping ALLAH because it gives you God-consciousness, and prevents you from doing evil deeds.

Al-Qur'an 2.21 O ye people! Adore your Guardian-Lord, who created you and those who came before you, that ye may become righteous

Also the Qur'an says that when mankind does good deeds, it is for his own benefit, not ALLAH's benefit.

Al-Qur'an 31.12 Any who is (so) grateful does so to profit his own soul: but if any is ungrateful, verily Allah is free of all wants, worthy of all praise

Al-Qur'an 17:7 If ye did well, ye did well for yourselves; if ye did evil, (ye did it) against yourselves

Obviously ALLAH doesn't need us to worship Him because it benefits Him, rather it benefits us because we are under a trial to sort out the righteous from the wrong-doers.

31. ALLAH WOULD NEVER HAVE A NON-MUSLIM IN PARADISE:

Not only do non-Muslims say this, there are even Muslims who say that this is true. They get this from certain verses of the Quran that they misinterpret such as:

Al-Qur'an 3:85 If anyone desires a religion other than Islam (submission to Allah), never will it be accepted of him; and in the Hereafter He will be in the ranks of those who have lost (All spiritual good)

Reading the verse by itself makes it seem pretty clear, but is it not that simple. Go back a few verses and it will become more clear who is being mentioned (Surah 3:81-82). These verses let the reader know that it is referring to "kafirs" (disbelievers), who have been given the message of Islam and know in the deepest part of their hearts that it's the truth, but still reject Islam.

Al-Qur'an 2:6 As to those who reject Faith, it is the same to them whether thou warn them or do nor warn them; they will not believe

It would be silly to say that all non-Muslims are kafirs because according to this verse, kafirs (those who reject faith) will never believe which is far from the truth with non-Muslims. There is a difference between a nonbeliever and a disbeliever. A non-believer does not believe in something. A disbeliever refuses to believe in something. A disbeliever has knowledge of the subject at hand, i.e. Al-Islam. A nonbeliever does not. So what if you never heard of Islam? Well those who were never given Dawah (invitation to Islam) they will not be punished.

Al-Quran 17:15 And we never punish until we sent a Messenger (to give warning)

Al-Qur'an 6:131 (The messengers were sent) thus, for thy Lord would not destroy for their wrong-doing men's habitations whilst their occupants were unwarned.

In fact, the Qur'an says they will be rewarded.

Al-Qur'an 2:62 Those who believe (in the Qur'an), and those who follow the Jewish (scriptures), and the Christians and the Sabians,- any who believe in Allah and the Last Day, and work righteousness, shall have their reward with their Lord; on them shall be no fear, nor shall they grieve.

Al-Qur'an 3:135-136 And those who, having done something to be ashamed of, or wronged their own *souls, earnestly bring Allah to mind, and ask for forgiveness for their sins,- and who can forgive sins except Allah?- and are never obstinate in persisting knowingly in (the wrong) they have done.*

For such the reward is forgiveness from their Lord, and Gardens with rivers flowing underneath,- an eternal dwelling: How excellent a recompense for those who work (and strive)!

32. ISLAM PROMOTES FORCED MARRIAGE:

This argument seems to be based on the fact that in some Muslims countries people force their sons/daughters into marriage. Although the Qur'an does give parents a role in setting up the marriage, nowhere in the Qur'an does it allow someone to force another into marriage. In fact, it says the exact opposite.

Al-Qur'an 4:19 O ye who believe! Ye are forbidden to inherit women against their will. Nor treat them with harshness

33. ISLAM KEEPS PEOPLE IGNORANT AND BACKWARDS:

When a person makes this assertion it almost sickens me because I assure you if you to go to the same person and ask them why any third-world country, that has little to no Islamic influence, is in the state that it is in they will say, "Oh, they're deprived of their natural resources" or "They just don't have the same benefits that we have." But when it comes to countries that are majority Muslim, they say "It is Islam." This argument fails because it simply using Al-Islam as a scapegoat. The Qur'an explicitly states that you should seek knowledge.

Al-Qur'an 20:114 O my lord! Advance me in knowledge

Al-Qur'an 39:9 Say: Are those equal, those who know and those who do not know? It is those who are endued with understanding that receive admonition.

So it can't possibly be the religion of Al-Islam that keeps some Muslim countries backwards. Obviously, if Al-Islam had such an influence on the economic and educational prosperity of a nation, they would be as successful as western countries. In fact, that has actually happened in the past while Europe was in the dark ages. Muslim countries were at the forefront of science, art, mathematics, technology, etc. Muslims also had a huge role in the renaissance. For example, there was a Spanish Muslim philosopher named Ibn Rushd (better known as Averroes), who contributed in the fields of music, medicine, philosophy, and Islamic theology. Even today, there are Muslim countries that are very successful. Saudi Arabia has an 82% literacy rate (much higher than it was in the pre-Islamic period), Malaysia has very little poverty and a 93% literacy rate, etc. There is no denying that there are other Muslim countries that need improvement and advancement, but Al-Islam is not the cause. It is the solution.

34. THE QUR'AN DOES NOT MENTIONED 5 DAILY PRAYERS:

Honestly I don't know what people are trying to prove when saying this about Al-Islam, but whatever it is, it's proven false by the following verse:

Qur'an 20.130 Therefore, be patient with what they say and celebrate the praises (constantly) of your lord Before the rising of the sun, and before it's setting; yea, celebrate them for part of the hours of the night, and at the two ends of the day: that thou mayest have (spiritual) joy

"Before the rising of the sun"=Fajr prayer
"Before it setting"= 'Asr prayer
"Parts of the hours of the night"= Isha prayer
"the two ends of the day"= Dhuhr and Maghrib prayers

35. MUSLIMS AREN'T PROMISED SALVATION:

In my opinion this argument is used by Christians, so they can get Muslim to convert by portraying Christianity as a relief because of their "assurance of salvation." Sadly what they fail to realize is the Qur'an does give us a means to earn salvation.

Qur'an 103:1-3 By (the token of) Time (through the ages)
Verily Man is in loss
Except such as have Faith, and do righteous deeds, and (join together) in the mutual teaching of truth, and of patience and constancy.

The idea of salvation is again expressed in the following verse:

Qur'an 66:6 O ye who believe! save yourselves and your families from a Fire whose fuel is Men and Stones, over which are (appointed) angels stern (and) severe, who flinch not (from executing) the Commands they receive from Allah, but do (precisely) what they are commanded.

Not only are Muslims saved according to the Qur'an, they have the ability to save themselves and others. This is an ability that those of the Christian faith believe is impossible. They are convinced that man is helpless to save himself and can only be saved by "the blood of Jesus." Their declaration of impotence is in spite of numerous passages of the Bible which correspond to this verse of the Qur'an. Al-Islam proclaims the power of man to hold his fate and destiny in his own hands. Just as he is able to perform wicked deeds earning him condemnation, he is also able to perform righteous deeds earning him salvation. Thus his salvation or damnation is based solely upon his belief, intentions and actions and no one else's.

36. A MARTYR GETS 72 VIRGINS IN HEAVEN:

The Qur'an does not say that a martyr will receive 72 virgins, thus this is not the reason that one becomes a martyr. In fact, you do not become a martyr on purpose. You are martyred by your enemy. Suicide is forbidden in Islam (Qur'an 2:195, 4:29). Murder is strictly forbidden in Islam. It is only permissible to kill someone in self-defense or in the requirements of justice and law for punishment (Qur'an 6:151).

The idea of martyrs and virgins is derived from the teaching in the Qur'an that one who dies in the way of ALLAH is granted Paradise. And in Paradise, those who are not married will have a "Houris" or companion who is described as pure and with large eyes. Because they are pure, those with a mind fixated on sex, think about virgins. And this is one aspect of the word "pure," but more appropriately, these companions are without sin. Also a man is not permitted to have more than 4 wives on earth. Muslims are not obliged to believe that ALLAH allows an indulgence, like 72 women in Paradise, when it is forbidden now.

37. MUSLIMS WORSHIP THE KAABA:

The Kaaba is the house of worship that Abraham and Ishmael (pbut) built in Mecca. They built it as a centerpiece for Muslims to worship GOD. Because Muslims around the world pray in unison towards this house of worship, many non-Muslims believe that Muslims are actually worshipping the structure as GOD. However the Kaaba is not considered GOD, or a symbol of GOD. As Muslims stand and bow, not one word is mentioned to or about the Kaaba. Every word is to GOD for the guidance and blessing of the individual and for others. Also Bilal stood on top of the Kaaba to give the Adhan. Clearly he did not worship it.

During Hajj, those Muslims who are close enough kiss the Kaaba. But kissing is not a means of worship. If so, we must also indict husbands and wives, and children and parents for kissing one another. Without doubt, that Muslims worship the Kaaba is a myth.

38. ISLAM PROMOTES SLAVERY:

When the word "slavery" is mentioned several descriptions and images appear in your mind. The inhumane practices of European and Arab "Muslims" in the Trans-Atlantic slave trade is not condone at all in Al-Islam. Those Muslims involved will surely face their Creator for the crimes that they committed. But the Qur'an does mention "people who my right hand possess." This description is for "prisoners of war," not our traditional idea of slaves.

Soldiers were captured in war and made to work in societies throughout history as a punishment for their crimes. This is what is mentioned in the Qur'an, prisoners of war, not slavery where people are kidnapped and forced to work indefinitely. And these prisoners of war are also to be set free according to the Qur'an, if there is any good in them (Qur'an 24:33)!
Al-Islam has a means of systemic manumission for these prisoners of war. What was practiced in America was totally criminal. It was brutal, savage, barbaric and complete oppression. And the Qur'an commands Muslims to fight the oppressor and fight for those oppressed. The Qur'an says that oppression is worse than death. Because of this principle and the obligation for all Muslims to study the Qur'an, forcing Al-Islam on slaves was not a good idea. This practice would surely backfire and cause the death of the slave owners. In fact, Muslims played a pivotal role in all of the slave revolts around the world. The notion of

obeying your slavemaster is not a tenet of Al-Islam as it is in other religions.

39. MUSLIMS CAN LIE TO NON-MUSLIMS:

Because terrorists represent a small fraction of Muslims, those who hate Al-Islam are forced to contrive another means to denigrate the other 99.98% of Muslims. These fear-mongers have made a huge deal about "Taqiyya." They say that Muslims can and are lying to non-Muslims about any and everything. Because people, who actually know Muslims, have nice things to say about them, it has become the goal of some to cast doubt and fear in the minds of all non-Muslims. The idea of "taqiyya" comes from this verse in the Qur'an:

Qur'an 16:106 Any one who, after accepting faith in Allah, utters Unbelief,- except under compulsion, his heart remaining firm in Faith - but such as open their breast to Unbelief, on them is Wrath from Allah, and theirs will be a dreadful Penalty.

Without doubt, the huge lie that is being told is exposed by reading the verse in question. It mentions that Muslims are permitted to renounce Al-Islam under compulsion. That means, if their life is in danger, they are allowed to say that they are not a Muslim when they really are. What person on earth would object to this? And if they do object, here is the kicker...Al-Islam also allows you to proclaim your religion and accept the consequence. As such, the

Muslim is a martyr and guaranteed Paradise. Thus ALLAH leaves it to the Muslim to decide whether to risk his or her life or not. But the verse in no way, justifies lying randomly to non-Muslims.

40. ISLAM VS JUDSIAM IS THE REASON FOR ISRAEL/PALESTINE CONFLICT:

There are some people who believe that the conflict in the Israel and the Palestinian Terrorities is a result of destiny or divine prophecy. Christian Dispensationalists view the conflict as a means of Jesus' (pbuh) return, so they allow and in some cases aid in the crimes committed to usher in the second coming. The Bible describes a teenage Ishmael mocking his younger brother Isaac (pbut). Some view this as an insight into the future relationship between their descendants since Ishmael is the father of the Arab people and Isaac (pbut) is the father of the Israelites. This notion gives rise to the idea that the tumult in this part of the world is due to a clash in their religions. But this is not the case. This is a political war over land. The Palestinians were living on the land and then it was made legal for every Jewish person on earth to move on their land. Their religions have little bearing on the conflict itself. Jews, Christians and Muslims were living there in peace and harmony until complete control was given to the extreme minority, the Jewish population. The land was classified as a Jewish State out of military might. Nonetheless, it is a fact that Muslims and Jews have lived in relative peace throughout their history. Oftentimes, Jews fled persecution from Christians into Muslim lands. Therefore the idea that Al-Islam is at the root of the Israel/Palestinian conflict is a myth.

41. A REFUTATION OF JUDAISM AND CHRISTIANITY IS A REFUTATION OF ISLAM:

It has become standard practice by some people to attack the tenets of Judaism or Christianity or both and upon successful refutation of them, suggests that Al-Islam is somehow defeated. They are under the impression that Judaism and Christianity are the root of Al-Islam, so it is unnecessary to even delve into the tenets of Al-Islam. This is a lazy and completely inaccurate approach. Al-Islam contains what is true in all religions, thus ones refutation of other religions will ultimately bring them closer to the truth of Al-Islam. Jews, Muslims and Christians believe in some of the same prophets, but this has no bearing on the validity on each religion. Because Jews do not accept all of the prophets that Christians accept and Christians do not accept all of the Prophets that Muslims accept. Nor do these groups have the same beliefs about these prophets. In short, Al-Islam is not in need of Judaism or Christianity. It stands firmly on its own merit.

42. AL-ISLAM HAS RELIGION, NOT SPIRITUALITY:

With the decline in followers of a particular religion, it has become common to attack Al-Islam as just a religion. Some maintain that one needs a relationship with GOD or one only needs a spiritual connection with GOD. As it pertains to a relationship with God, this often mean that they don't have to follow all of the rules like Muslims do. They simply believe and they are saved. Well belief is nothing without action. James, Jesus' (pbuh) brother according to the Bible, said "Faith without works is dead!" And Muslims have both faith and good deeds. The relationship that we have with GOD is one of Creator and servant. Our service is our righteous deeds.

This brings us to the point of spirituality. In the word "spirituality" is the word "spirit." Our spirit is the immaterial driving force within us. It is our true self; our soul. That immaterial self comes from the immaterial Creator. We connect with Him through our immaterial thoughts, immaterial feelings and immaterial intentions. These thoughts, feelings and intentions are personified through our physical body and its actions. The Qur'an says that we purifies or stain our own soul, through our actions. That means that our spirituality comes from our service to others for the sake of God. Who is more in tune with GOD than a person who is GOD conscience in all of his actions? Simply following the tenets of Al-Islam makes the Muslim the most spiritual person on earth.

43. AL-ISLAM ERASES CULTURE:

My Imam said if Prophet Muhammad (pbuh) was born in Alaska, he would be dressed as an Eskimo. And that struck a chord with me because it made me think about Muslims all over the world who believe that dressing as Arab's do or did makes them more like Prophet Muhammad (pbuh). In its simplest form, it is true. But the goal is not to dress like him, but to be like him. Be righteous as he was and be practical as he was. Dress as he would, if he were born where you were born. Act as he would act, if he lived in the same time and under the same circumstances that you are in. Arabia, like Alaska, has extreme weather, so dressing with the same garbs in other parts of the world is not practical.

If following the Sunnah of Prophet Muhammad (pbuh) meant doing everyday things as he does, then we all should get rid of our cars and ride a camel, live in Arabia, marry a woman named Khadijah, chose merchant trader as our profession, etc. We are individuals, who were born in different societies, communities and with different cultures. We cannot divorce ourselves from our culture. There may be aspects of our culture which conflict with Al-Islam and they should be eschewed, but Al-Islam is not meant to be completely monolithic. The pillars and tenets of Al-Islam will never change, but ones culture can coexist with Al-Islam without comprising the religion.

44. HELL IS ETERNAL:

There is a prevailing assumption that hell is infinite. The duration of a person's time of hell is better described as indefinite, than infinite. The Qur'an often mentions the torment of hell to be forever, but this may be used as a measure for deterring man from sin. Along with the horrid images of hell is the idea that it is a never ending punishment. But the Qur'an also says that the people of hell will dwell therein for AGES (78:23). As in other references of time in the Qur'an, this is in respect to man's perception of the time spent in hell, thus it is relative. Hell may seem to last forever due to man's disposition inside of it, but it may very well just be a very long time for him. To add to this notion, on at least two occasions, the Qur'an says they will dwell in hell forever, EXCEPT as ALLAH wills (6:128, 11:107). There are perhaps some who deserve everlasting punishment and others who deserve relief from the punishment. The possibility that one can dwell in such a place without release is what is meant to keep man from following this path. But ALLAH has left the slight chance for relief, but who wants to take that chance?

The fact that hell has different degrees and levels might also be an indicator that hell is not literally forever, or not forever for everyone inside of hell. If there is a lowest level and a more harsh degree of hell, then there is a highest level and the least harsh degree of hell. In the prison system, there are the most dangerous offenders and those who are less dangerous. Obviously, the least dangerous person is closer to relief than the most dangerous prisoner is. And the least dangerous offender is more likely to be considered for release. This would explain the verses of Surah 7 which illustrate the life of hell and ironically interjects the probability of such a person to enter paradise (7:38-41). Though it pronounces the improbability of such an event happening, considering all the benevolence given to man while on earth, it is not impractical or impossible for GOD to do.

According to traditions attributed to the Prophet Muhammad (pbuh), there will be Muslims who go to hell, but no one who believes that there is no GOD but ALLAH and that Muhammad is his messenger, will remain in hell. Most Muslims believe this tradition to be authentic and it is actually a claim which helps substantiate the notion that one's stay in hell is indefinite, not infinite.

45. THE QUR'AN DEFINES THE TRINITY AS THE FATHER, THE MOTHER AND THE SON:

Al-Quran 5:116 And behold! Allah will say: "O Jesus the son of Mary! Didst thou say unto men, worship me and my mother as gods in derogation of Allah?" He will say: "Glory to Thee! never could I say what I had no right (to say). Had I said such a thing, thou wouldst indeed have known it

It has been the tactic of several evangelists to suggest that the author of the Qur'an mistook the Trinity to be "the father, the mother and the son." They make this pronouncement because of verses like the one shown above, which denounce the worship of Jesus (pbuh) and Mary. But there are several problems with this claim. First, the Qur'an does not define the components of Trinity. This is only their assumption that the Trinity is composed in this manner in the Qur'an. And how can they criticize the Qur'an for not describing the Trinity, when the Bible does not define or describe it? The Trinity is an evolved doctrine and the Holy spirit was the last part of the godhead to be fully established. And both, Jesus and the Holy spirit were established by people hundreds of years after the after the life of Jesus (pbut). Though most Christians believe that the Trinity is well-defined and established doctrine in the Bible, it is no were to be found.

Al-Qur'an 3:78 There is among them a section who distort the Book with their tongues. (As they read) you would think it is a part of the Book, but it is no part of the Book; and they say, "That is from Allah," but it is not from Allah: It is they who tell a lie against Allah, and (well) they know it!

The Qur'an denounces all forms of the Trinity including the worship of Jesus (pbuh) and Mary as God. It is well known that there are Christians today who pay homage and submit their prayers to the Virgin Mary. And there were Christians in Arabia in the time of Prophet Muhammad (pbuh), who worshipped Mary called Collyridians. She is seen as the Mother of GOD. This idea may seem outrageous, but if we are to believe that she nurtured GOD Almighty for 9 months and raised him to adulthood, then the Collyridians' conclusion seems inevitable. Also, the doctrines of the Trinity have undergone great changes throughout history, thus it is possible to change again. So how can the Trinitarian possibly indict someone for misrepresenting the Trinity? It is actually advantageous for the Qur'an not to define the Trinity as it may be altered AGAIN. Not to mention that the Qur'an says don't worship two gods (16:51), as well as three (4:171). What do they suggest that this means? It is clear that the Quran is dismissing the idea of any number of gods, besides one.

46. THE ISLAMIC VIEW OF PROPHETS IS THE SAME AS THE JUDEO-CHRISTIANS' VIEW:

The Qur'an states that prophets were sent to every people (16:36). God is not fixated only on one group of people.

Though Prophet Muhammad (pbuh) is to guide the whole of humanity and he is the last prophet, the Qur'an is adamant that Muslims are to make no distinction between the prophets of Islam (2:136, 285, 3:84, 4:152). Despite an effort to combat the reverence other religious people have for their prophets, it seems Muslims often fall victim to exalting Prophet Muhammad (pbuh) above other prophets. Though ALLAH gives different prophets different gifts and honors (2:253), it is ALLAH who may distinguish between the honor due a particular prophet over another. Because one prophet is more successful than another is no ground to exalt one over the other. All their messages come from the same source, but it is the people who decide whether to believe or not. The miracles one works does not determine their status in Al-Islam, either. Different circumstances call for different means to convey and convince. In the end, the words and deeds done by a prophet is from ALLAH, thus the distinction is impossible, because you are comparing ALLAH'S gift with ALLAH'S gift.

In the Bible, seemingly ever prophet is guilty of some major offense to the laws of GOD and the laws of decency. The Muslim is told in the Qur'an, that

prophets are men of exemplary behavior. They are pious and devout and fearful of ALLAH, more so than anyone of their nation. This is why they were chosen by ALLAH. Armed with the CRITERION, Muslims can easily sift through the Bible and find the story of the drunkenness of Noah, the curse of Noah, the incest of Abraham, Jacob wrestling God, Moses' blasphemy, Aaron's idolatry, Elisha causing two bears to kill 42 children for teasing his bald-head, Ezekiel eating human feces, David's murder and adultery, Solomon's harem and Jesus (pbut) calling a sick child a dog as innovations used by the enemies of these prophets. We cannot accept that GOD chose such people to lead mankind.

47. MUSLIMS AND MUHAMMAD (PBUH) DON'T HAVE A PROMISE OF HEAVEN:

Very similar to the promise of salvation, Christians often ask for assurance for Muslims that they will enter Heaven. They surmise that because Muslims not only believe but work to earn a place in Paradise, then they are not certain whether they will enter Paradise or not. However the Qur'an contradicts their ideas.

Surah 19:61 Gardens of Eternity, those which (Allah) Most Gracious has promised to His servants in the Unseen: for His promise must (necessarily) come to pass.

Surah 9:72 Allah hath promised to Believers, men and women, gardens under which rivers flow, to dwell therein, and beautiful mansions in gardens of everlasting bliss.

As you can see, believers are guaranteed Paradise from ALLAH. The criteria are righteousness and repentance for wickedness.

Now let's go to the hadith by the Prophet (pbuh) to see what he had to say on his place in the afterlife. It is recorded in *Sahih Muslim: Kitab Al-zuhd wa Al-Raqa'iq* by Abu Huraira that the Prophet (pbuh) said,

"One who looks after the orphan whether he is his relative or not, I and he would be together in Paradise"

48. MUSLIMS WANT TO IMPOSE SHARIA LAW ON NON-MUSLIMS:

This is another ploy by anti-Islam propagandists to strike fear in non-Muslims. The first problem with their claim is that they define Sharia Law. I would like to know how and with what authority do these non-scholarly, non-Muslims definitively say what Islamic law is, when actual Muslims and actual scholars of Al-Islam, all over the world, disagree on what laws should be. Whenever you hear a non-Muslim start listing the tenets of Sharia Law, beware and be cautious in accepting their word for something studied and argued over for over 1000 years by Muslims who are sincerely trying to get it right. Sharia literally means street or way and throughout the world Muslims use the knowledge of learned people and consensus in their land to determine their "way."

The second problem is that Muslims are not trying to impose their law or their religion on anyone. To the surprise of some non-Muslims, Muslims really believe in the Qur'an and they want to live by it, unlike some of other religions. When Muslims has a large enough community, they establish their way within the confines of that community. Because this is done, some people maintain that Muslims want to subjugate the world and make them submit to Islamic law. This is not the case. There is no compulsion in Al-Islam. Your desire to be a Muslim, to follow the tenets of Al-Islam, and to live by the Qur'an and the Sunnah of Prophet Muhammad (pbuh) is your choice.

49. WHAT MUSLIMS DO IS WHAT AL-ISLAM TEACHES:

This is one of the greatest obstacles for Muslims today. Culture and religion are at times so blurred that they are indistinguishable. When the media outlets show a Muslim doing anything, it is perceived to be a tenet of Al-Islam. Female genital mutilation, honor killings, and the 2nd class treatment of women have no root in Al-Islam, but some Muslims indulge in these practices. The kissing while greeting, particular clothing, and even the symbols used to represent Al-Islam are from Muslims but not rooted in Al-Islam. This is not to say that they are prohibited, but it is to say that they are not required for one to be a practicing Muslims. Therefore it is very important to distinguish Al-Islam from Muslims practice. If it cannot be found in the authentic sources of inspiration and revelation, it is not a part of Al-Islam no matter how many Muslims perform or practice it.

50. ISLAM IS NOT THE TRUTH:

Why are there so many myths and misunderstandings about Al-Islam? And are these just misunderstandings or are they intentional? There is no doubt that many Muslims and non-Muslims have spread falsehoods about Al-Islam without malicious intent. And it also without doubt that many people have intentionally misled others about Al-Islam. There are a multitude of people who know the truth, but they allow people to believe in myths. We should consider why that is. Why would there be so many lies about Al-Islam? Why are these lies widespread without them being corrected? More importantly, if Al-Islam is untrue, why are so many myths about Al-Islam necessary? Who proves that something is false, by using false evidence?

People lie in order to conceal the truth. They lie because a lie is more beneficial to them than the truth is. Yet the truth can only harm someone who is lying. There is an old saying, "All that glistens isn't gold." Well it is also true that not all gold glistens. Sometimes you have to uncover the treasure because it is deeply buried in myths and misconceptions.

Al-Qur'an 61:8 Their intention is to extinguish Allah's Light with their mouths. But Allah will complete (the revelation of) His Light, even though the Unbelievers may detest (it).

Al-Qur'an 61:9 It is He Who has sent His Messenger with Guidance and the Religion of Truth, that he may proclaim it over all religion, even though the Pagans may detest (it).

Take another look at the Religion of Truth. Al-Islam is our natural way of life. It is natural for man to be righteous, to be brotherly/sisterly, to be a good husband or wife, to be a good friend, to be a good neighbor, and to be a good Samaritan. It is natural for man to fight oppression and fight for the oppressed. It is natural for man to give to charity and to help those in need. All these things are what make a good Muslim. This is GOD's will for man and when you perform these actions, you are in a state of Al-Islam.

Al-Islam's every tenet calls for a closeness with GOD. When you embrace Al-Islam, you embrace your true self and your true purpose in life. When one concludes that there is a GOD, who can find fault with a system which provides a constant reminder of GOD? This life is but a test for man. GOD has given him a soul. He has given man intelligence, and understanding. GOD has given man a conscience, serving as a compass to lead us towards righteousness. GOD has given man, through his Prophets, examples of how one should lead a pious life and GOD has given man opportunity. Every day that you live, every moment of every day, you are provided an opportunity to seek truth, embrace and accept truth and live truth. Come and explore the truth from GOD given to all of mankind and to all of his creation, AL-ISLAM.

FIVE PILLARS OF ISLAM

1. Shahadah- This is the oath that every person must say and believe in order to be a Muslim. It is as follows: I bear witness that there is no god, but ALLAH and I bear witness that Muhammad is his Messenger. This is the most important tenants of Islam. Islam is vehement in its insistence that God is one, without partners or associates and this God (in Arabic ALLAH) communicates his will to mankind through exemplary men in history. These men are Prophets and/or Messengers of God and they include Adam, Abraham, Noah, Jacob, Isaac, Ishmael, Moses, Aaron, Lot, David, Solomon and Jesus (pbut). The last of the Prophets of God is Muhammad (pbuh) and he has been given a message to convey to all of humanity. That message is the same message given by all of God's prophets, submission to the will of God. The Arabic word for submission to God's will is Islam.

2. Worship- called Salat in Arabic; it is the prayer Muslims give to God/ALLAH five times a day. It is not the traditional prayer of requests for God. It is structured for the praise and remembrance of God throughout the day.

3. Charity- called Zakat in Arabic; it is the obligation on every Muslim to give 2.5% of his wealth to the poor, the sick and for travelers in need. God gives people opportunities to help others. One of these opportunities is with one's wealth, but it also includes sharing your time and effort to help others. In fact, a smile or a kind word is an act of charity and worship in Islam.

4. Fasting-During the month of Ramadhan, all Muslims are required to restrict their consumption of food and drink from sunrise to sunset. They also abstain from sexual relations with their spouse from sunrise to sunset. This is a lesson in self-restraint and a way in which one can feel the struggle of those less-fortunate. This is also a time to reacquaint one's self with the Qur'an and to renew their commitment to following the decrees set forth in Islam.

5. Hajj- This is the largest pilgrimage in the world. It is a pilgrimage to the holy city of Mecca and it is required of all able bodied Muslims, who can afford it, at least once in their life. Every Muslim, whether rich or poor, black or white, short or tall are all brothers and sisters. We all pray in unison in one direction, at the same time and using the similar words in praise to God and this pilgrimage is the ultimate manifestation of the oneness of the 1.8 billion Muslim community.

ABOUT THE AUTHOR

Mr. Campbell, now Ismael Bilal Saleem, was raised attending both the Christian Church and the Muslim Mosque. He was always inquisitive about religion. Around the age of 14, he decided that Al-Islam was the path for him. However, he was rather secretive about his belief due to the negative perception many had of the religion. When Al-Islam became the topic of any discussion, he maintained the Islamic sympathizer role as the son of a Muslim, while being careful not to be identified as a Muslim himself. The stigma surrounding Al-Islam and Muslims only intensified throughout the years, but so too did his desire to announce to the world that AL-ISLAM IS THE TRUTH. Throughout his life, he had engage others in discussions on religion and a little over three years ago he realized that the issues that were raised in debate and in dialogue were issues which warranted extensive details, evidence and explanations. Drawing from all the books, lectures, and debates he come in contact with, and all the talks with Muslims, Christians, Jews, Hindus, atheists and agnostics, he set out to write one book which would convince all of the truth about the God of the universe. This one book blossomed into eight books which are written with the primary goal of proving the validity of Al Islam. It is with his sincerest effort that he wrote these books, with the hope that all readers will set aside their preconceived ideas and have an open mind.

BOOKS BY THIS AUTHOR INCLUDE:

1. ISLAM IS THE TRUTH

2. JESUS WAS NOT CRUCIFIED

3. THE JEWISH TORAH IS NOT THE WORD OF GOD

4. THERE IS NO TRINITY

5. 50 MYTHS ABOUT ISLAM

6. GOD THE IRRESISTIBLE

7. FAQs ABOUT ISLAM

8. WHAT GOD SAYS ABOUT JESUS

9. THE MOST IMPORTANT THING IN THE WORLD

10. THE SOLUTION

11. THE UNADULTERATED TRUTH ABOUT THE PALESTINIAN/ISRAELI CONFLICT

12. RACE AND RELIGION

For information on Ismael Bilal Saleem's Books, Lectures and Spoken Word visit:

Website: Islamisthetruth.org

Facebook: Ismael Bilal Saleem-I.D. Campbell

Youtube: onlygodisgod

Twitter: @MrIDCampbell

Made in the USA
Columbia, SC
26 March 2018